HOW TO DRAW PIRATES

DISCARD

David Antram

PowerKiDS press™

New York

Published in 2012 by The Rosen Publishing Group, Inc.
29 East 21st Street, New York, NY 10010

Editor: Rob Walker
U.S. Editor: Kara Murray

Library of Congress Cataloging-in-Publication Data

Antram, David, 1958-
  How to draw pirates / by David Antram. — 1st ed.
      p. cm. — (How to draw)
  Includes index.
  ISBN 978-1-4488-4515-6 (library binding) — ISBN 978-1-4488-4520-0 (pbk.) —
  ISBN 978-1-4488-4526-2 (6-pack)
  1. Pirates in art—Juvenile literature.
  2. Drawing—Technique—Juvenile literature. I. Title.
  NC825.P57A58 2012
  741.2—dc22

                              2010051196

Manufactured in Heshan, China

CPSIA Compliance Information: Batch #SS1102PK: For Further Information contact
Rosen Publishing, New York, New York at 1-800-237-9932

PAPER FROM
SUSTAINABLE
FORESTS

Contents

4   Making a Start

6   Perspective

8   Drawing Tools

10   Materials

12   Pirate Hats

14   Blackbeard

16   Pirate Flags

18   Pirate Trio

20   Buccaneer

22   Pirate Ships

24   Pirate with Parrot

26   Pirates in Action

28   Treasure Maps

30   Pirate in the Rigging

32   Glossary, Index, and Web Sites

Making a Start

Learning to draw is about looking and seeing. Keep practicing and get to know your subject. Use a sketchbook to make quick drawings. Start by doodling and experimenting with shapes and patterns. There are many ways to draw. This book shows only some methods. Visit art galleries, look at artists' drawings, see how friends draw, but above all, find your own way.

Use simple shapes to draw the figures in action.

Remember that practice makes perfect. If it looks wrong, start again. Keep working at it. The more you draw, the more you will learn.

Perspective

If you look at any object from different viewpoints, you will see that the part that is closest to you looks larger, and the part farthest away from you looks smaller.

Drawing in perspective is a way of creating a feeling of space, of showing three dimensions on a flat surface.

V.P.

The vanishing point (V.P.) is the place in a perspective drawing where parallel lines appear to meet. The position of the vanishing point depends on the viewer's eye level. Sometimes a low viewpoint can give your drawing added drama.

Two-point perspective uses two vanishing points. One for lines running along the length of the object, and one on the opposite side for lines running across the width of the object.

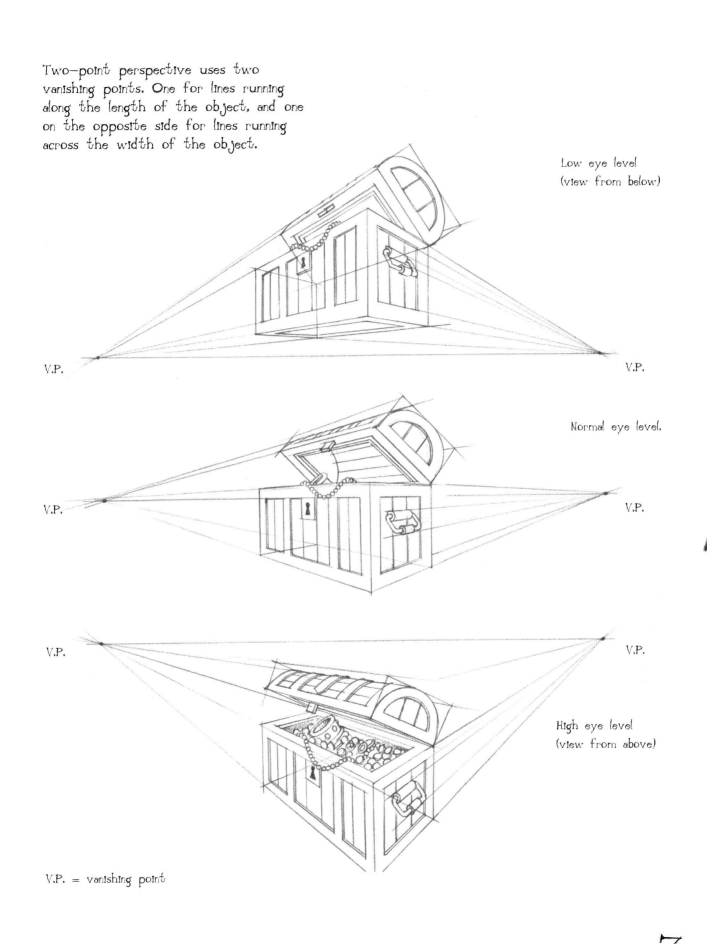

Low eye level
(view from below)

V.P.

V.P.

Normal eye level.

V.P.

V.P.

V.P.

V.P.

High eye level
(view from above)

V.P. = vanishing point

7

Drawing Tools

ere are just a few of the many tools that you can use for drawing. Let your imagination go and have fun experimenting with all the different marks you can make.

Pencil

Watercolor pencil

Charcoal pencil

Charcoal stick

Pastels

Finger painting

Black, gray, and white pastel on gray construction paper

Each grade of **pencil** makes a different mark, from fine, gray lines to soft, black ones. Hard pencils are graded from #2½ to #4 (the hardest). A #2 pencil is ideal for general sketching. A #1 pencil is a soft pencil. It makes the softest and blackest lines.

Watercolor pencils come in many different colors and make a line similar to a #2 pencil. But paint over your finished drawing with clean water, and the lines will soften and run.

It is less messy and easier to get a fine line with a **charcoal pencil** than a stick of charcoal. Create soft tones by smudging lines with your finger. **Ask an adult** to spray the drawing with fixative to prevent further smudging.

Pastels are brittle sticks of powdered color. They blend and smudge easily and are ideal for quick sketches. Pastel drawings work well on textured, colored paper. **Ask an adult** to spray your finished drawing with fixative.

Experiment with **finger painting**. Your fingerprints make exciting patterns and textures. Use your fingers to smudge soft pencil, charcoal, and pastel lines.

8

Ballpoint pens are very useful for sketching and making notes. Make different tones by building up layers of shading.

A **mapping pen** has to be dipped into bottled ink to fill the nib. Different nib shapes make different marks. Try putting a diluted ink wash over parts of the finished drawing.

Draftsman's pens and specialist **art pens** can produce very fine lines and are ideal for creating surface texture. A variety of pen nibs are available which produce different widths of line.

Felt-tip pens are ideal for quick sketches. If the ink is not waterproof, try drawing on wet paper and see what happens.

Broad-nibbed **marker pens** make interesting lines and are good for large, bold sketches. Try using a black pen for the main sketch and a gray one to block in areas of shadow.

Paintbrushes are shaped differently to make different marks. Japanese brushes are soft and produce beautiful, flowing lines. Large sable brushes are good for painting a wash over a line drawing. Fine brushes are good for drawing delicate lines.

Ballpoint pen

Mapping pen

Draftsman's pen

Felt-tip pen

Marker pen

Paintbrush

9

Materials

Try using different types of drawing paper and materials. Experiment with charcoal, wax crayons, and pastels. All pens, from felt-tips to ballpoints, will make interesting marks. You could also try drawing with pen and ink on wet paper.

Felt-tips come in a range of line widths. The wider pens are good for filling in large areas of flat tone.

Silhouette is a style of drawing that mainly uses solid black shapes.

Ink silhouette

Lines drawn in **ink** cannot be erased, so keep your ink drawings sketchy and less rigid. Don't worry about mistakes as these lines can be lost in the drawing as it develops.

Hatching

Adding light and shade to a drawing with an ink pen can be tricky. Use a solid layer of ink for the very darkest areas and cross—hatching (straight lines criss—crossing each other) for ordinary dark tones. Hatching (straight lines running parallel to each other) can be used for midtones. Leave the lightest areas white.

Pencil drawings can include a vast amount of detail and tone. Try experimenting with different grades of pencil to get a range of light and shade effects in your drawing.

Remember the best equipment and materials will not necessarily make the best drawing. Only practice will.

11

Pirate Hats

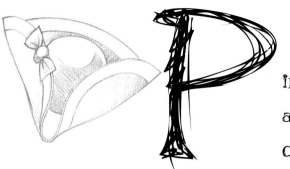

Pirates wear a variety of hats with different shapes and styles. Hats are best constructed along with the head so that they fit snugly together.

The style of a hat or headdress can make one character very different from another. Onboard the ship, the style of hat can denote status.

Drawing a hat and head together helps you understand how the hat fits around the head.

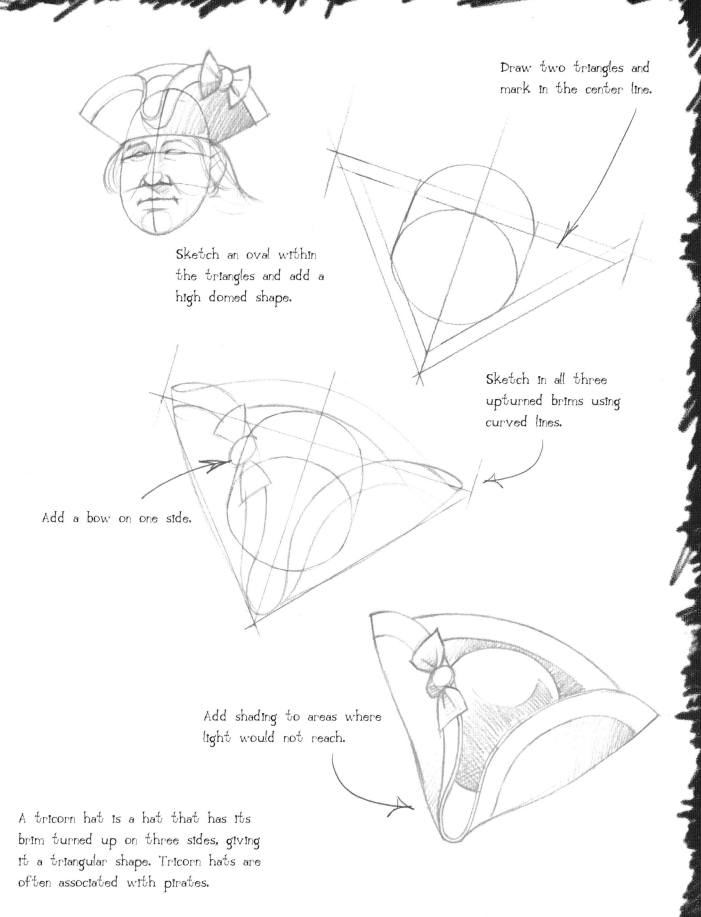

Draw two triangles and mark in the center line.

Sketch an oval within the triangles and add a high domed shape.

Sketch in all three upturned brims using curved lines.

Add a bow on one side.

Add shading to areas where light would not reach.

A tricorn hat is a hat that has its brim turned up on three sides, giving it a triangular shape. Tricorn hats are often associated with pirates.

Remove any unwanted construction lines.

13

Blackbeard

Blackbeard was a fearsome pirate who terrorized all who sailed the Caribbean Sea. He carried six loaded pistols and famously tucked smoldering lit fuses under his hat so that the smoke would make him look even scarier.

Draw ovals for the head, body, and hips.

Head

Add straight lines for the shoulders and hips.

Body

Hips

Add the arms and legs with dots to show the joints.

Add ears and facial details.

Draw ovals for the knees.

Sketch simple shapes for the hands and feet.

Draw the shape of the musket.

Add shape to the feet.

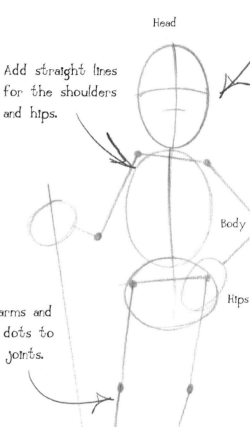

14

Draw the shape of the hat and clothing.

Sketch in the beard, mustache, and hair.

Sketch the sword and pistols.

Finish the beard and add shading.

Add details to the musket.

Add the shape of the shoes.

Shade all areas where light would not reach.

Finish off all the details of the clothing. Add ragged edges and tears.

Add detail to his weapons.

Add buckles to his shoes and complete all details.

Remember to remove any unwanted construction lines.

15

Pirate Flags

Hoist the Jolly Roger! The skull and crossbones flag struck terror into all seafarers. Each pirate captain had his own version of the Jolly Roger to identify his ship.

Draw an arm and hand shape.

Thomas Tew's flag

Now add the fingers clutching a curved cutlass.

Shade in the background.

Henry Avery's flag

Draw the side view of a skull. Add crossbones.

Stede Bonnet's flag

Draw in a pirate and a skeleton.

Bartholomew Roberts's flag

Shade in the backgrounds.

16

Calico Jack Rackham's flag

Sketch a billowing flag. Draw in a skull (front view) and then two crossed swords.

Shade in the background.

Now practice drawing the same design but on different flag shapes.

Negative Space
Look at the shapes left between the lines of your drawing. This can help you spot mistakes.

Remember to lose sections of the image where the fabric turns or hangs.

17

Pirate Trio

Sketch in ovals for the heads, bodies, and hips.

This character doesn't look too happy. Has he been taken prisoner or are his shipmates giving him a helping hand? This pose captures the sense that the other two are supporting his weight.

Use straight lines to position the arms and legs with dots for joints.

Indicate the direction of each head by sketching the position of the facial features.

Add simple shapes for the hands and feet.

Draw ovals for the knees.

Draw tube shapes for the arms and legs.

18

Sketch the pirate's headwear.

Draw the ears and facial features.

Start to draw the main shapes of the clothing and shoes.

Finish off all details to the clothes and heads.

Add detail to areas of their clothes, such as striped socks.

The sagging tunic adds weight to the body.

Shade in areas where light would not reach.

19

Buccaneer

Armed to the teeth, this cutthroat pirate is ready to attack. This pose captures a sense of action and excitement.

Sketch ovals for the head, body, and hips. Add straight lines for the shoulders and hips.

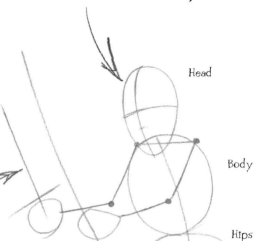

Head

Body

Hips

Add shapes for hands and feet.

Draw straight lines for the arms and legs.

Add lines for a cutlass in one hand and a dagger in the other.

Draw the hat around the head.

Use curved lines to add shape to the blades. Draw in handles.

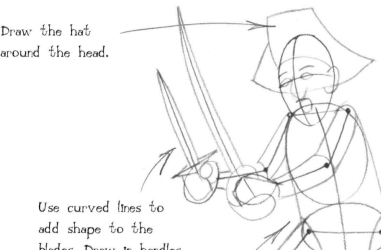

Add the ears and position the facial features.

Using the construction lines as a guide, start drawing the main shapes of the body.

Sketch tube shapes for the arms and legs with dots for joints.

Add more shape to the feet.

Add detail to the structure of the hat.

Draw hair using flowing lines.

Draw the eyes, nose, ears, and mouth.

Add the fingers and thumbs.

Use curved, sweeping lines to draw the swirl of the topcoat to show movement.

Draw in cuffs on sleeves.

Add large cuffs to the top of the boots.

Add shading to the hat and belt.

Complete the details of the cutlass and dagger.

Add pockets, buttonholes, buttons, and patterned cuffs.

Shade all the areas where light would not reach.

Add buckles to the boots.

21

Pirate Ships

Pirate ships were generally small, fast ships like sloops that were easy to maneuver. Large merchant ships tended to be heavier and slower so they were easy targets for pirates to attack.

Add three lines for the masts.

Draw a long, boxlike shape on two levels for the ship's hull.

See pages 6–7 to put perspective into use.

Using a high vanishing point, draw the sails.

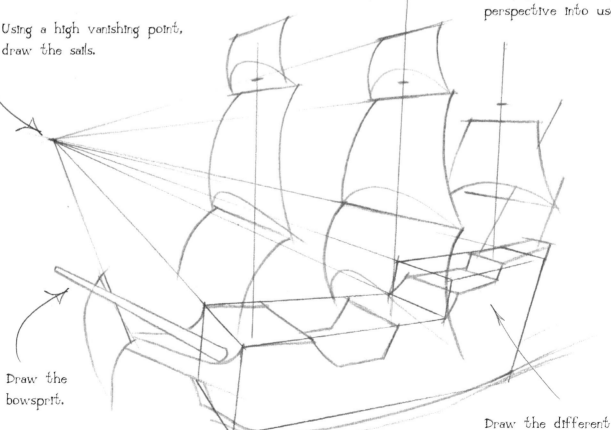

Draw the bowsprit.

Draw the different deck levels.

22

Start sketching in the ship's details now.

Draw a center line through the sails.

Draw straight lines for the rigging.

Composition

By framing your drawing with a square or a rectangle, you can make it look completely different.

Add a flag at the rear.

Add lines along the shape of the hull to define it.

Finish off the detail on the rigging and add masts and rails.

Add detail to the sails.

Draw a skull and crossbones on the flag.

Draw the decking.

Add cannon ports.

Pirate with Parrot

The exotic animals that pirates found as they traveled around the world made excellent companions onboard the ship. Parrots could even mimic speech!

Draw an oval for the head.

Draw a vertical ellipse through the center of the oval.

Draw a horizontal ellipse through the center of the oval to position the eyes.

Add the nose, mouth, and ears.

Draw ovals for the parrot's head and body.

Sketch the shoulders using curved lines.

Sketch the parrot's eyes, beak, and wings.

Add detail to the pirate's facial expression.

Draw in more shape to the parrot's head.

Add eyes and markings.

Draw the bandana.

Finish off facial details.

Sketch the pirate's clothing.

Use small, broken lines to create feathers.

Add tone with shading.

Shade in any areas where light would not reach.

25

Pirates in Action

Pirates relied on speed and terror to attack their victim's ship. Once onboard they fought with great fury. This action pose captures the cut and thrust of the attack.

Draw ovals for the head, body, and hips of both figures.

Sketch the straight lines for the arms and legs with dots for joints.

Sketch straight lines for the weapons.

Add simple shapes for the hands and feet.

Note the angle of the feet.

Position the eyes, nose, and ears.

Using the construction lines as a guide, draw the main shapes of the bodies.

Draw the tube shapes for the arms and legs.

Add fingers and thumbs to the hands.

Add details to the weapons.

Draw the hat shapes curving around the head.

Sketch large cuffs on the coat.

Add tall boots that go over the knee.

Draw boots with a fold over the top.

Add detail to the faces and hair.

Draw all the finishing details on the clothing and boots.

Finish off the daggers and swords.

Add detail to the faces and hair.

Add shading to the areas that light would not reach.

Add buckles.

Remove any unwanted construction lines.

Treasure Maps

In pirate stories. X marks the spot where the treasure is buried. In real life, the maps were the real treasure. Knowledge of an area meant the pirates could take their prey by surprise and then quickly disappear again.

Draw a rectangle.

Sketch three small circles and a cross.

Add a small circle with a vertical and horizontal line through it.

Start sketching land shapes and islands.

Draw borders inside the rectangle.

Sketch inner rings to the circle.

Add decorative features like palm trees, ships, sea monsters, and dolphins.

Add curled-up corners and tears.

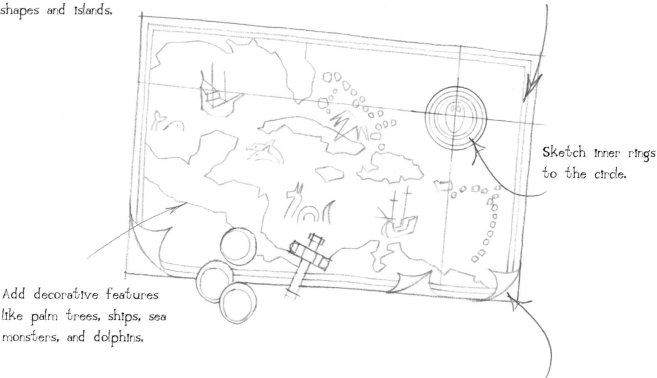

28

Draw more detail on the ships and monsters.

Add more rips and tears. Sketch a pattern in the border.

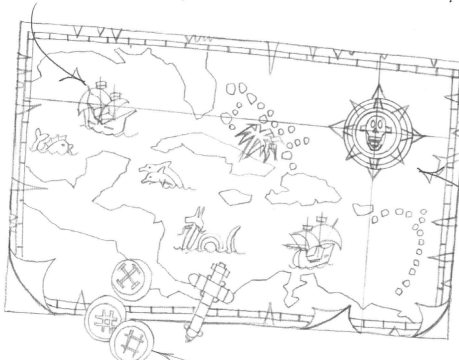

Add a skull and points to the compass.

Add more detail to the cross and the pieces of eight.

Alternate mid-range tones and dark tones on the border.

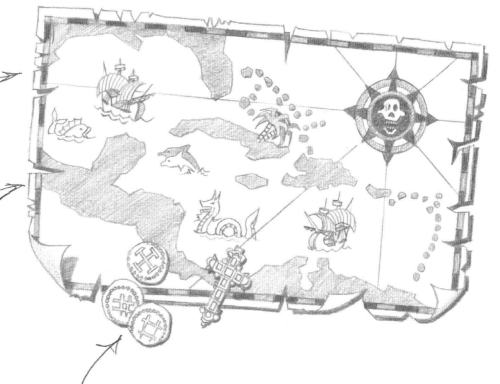

Add tone by shading all the landmasses.

Complete all the details on the small drawings.

29

Pirate in the Rigging

As the cannons roar, this pirate scrambles up the rigging to assess the attack. "All hands on deck! Get your swords and pistols — battle stations, everyone!" This pirate figure is ready for action.

Sketch ovals for the head, body, and hips.

Draw straight lines for the rigging.

Add a line for the cutlass.

Head

Body

Hips

Add the hat shape and position the eyes, ear, nose, and mouth.

Draw the curved lines of the cutlass.

Draw the hand shapes clutching the rigging and the sword.

Using construction lines as a guide, draw the main shapes of the body.

Use straight lines to position the arms and the legs with dots for the joints.

Sketch circles and loops for the cross ropes.

Draw tube shapes for the arms and legs. Add ovals for the knees.

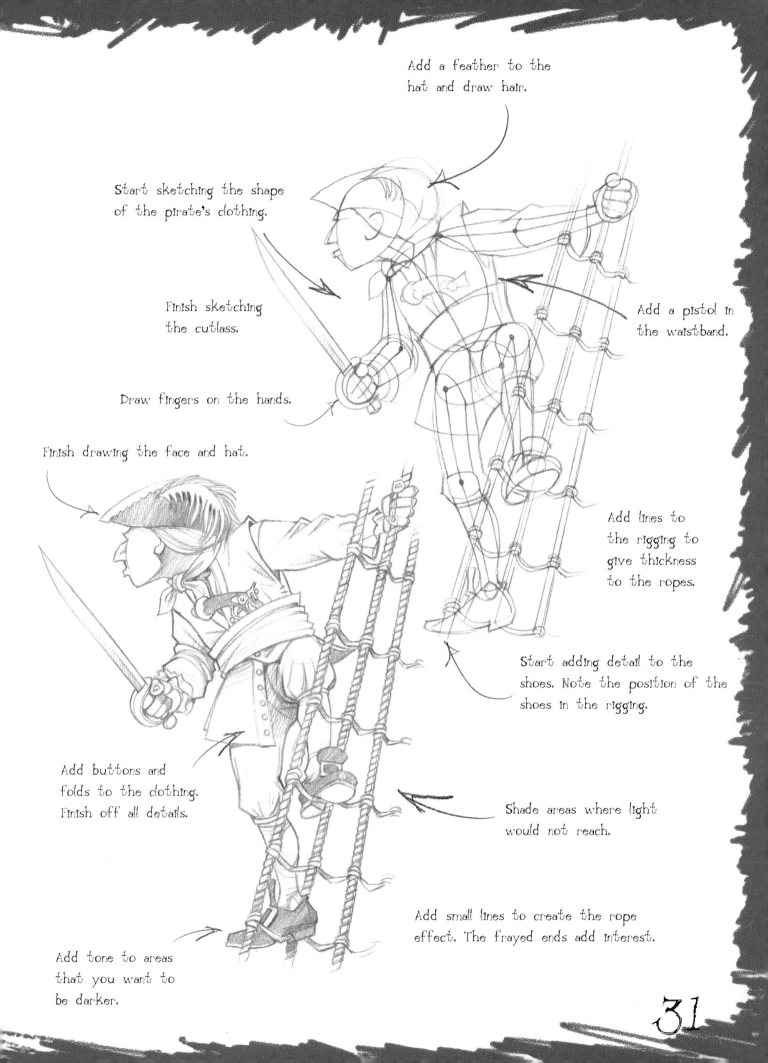

Add a feather to the hat and draw hair.

Start sketching the shape of the pirate's clothing.

Finish sketching the cutlass.

Draw fingers on the hands.

Finish drawing the face and hat.

Add a pistol in the waistband.

Add lines to the rigging to give thickness to the ropes.

Start adding detail to the shoes. Note the position of the shoes in the rigging.

Add buttons and folds to the clothing. Finish off all details.

Shade areas where light would not reach.

Add small lines to create the rope effect. The frayed ends add interest.

Add tone to areas that you want to be darker.

31

Glossary

bowsprit (BOW-sprit) A pole that extends forward from the front of a ship.

composition (kom-puh-ZIH-shun) The arrangement of the parts of a picture on the drawing paper.

construction lines (kun-STRUK-shun LYNZ) Guidelines used in the early stages of a drawing. They are usually erased later.

galleries (GA-luh-reez) Rooms or buildings that show works of art.

negative space (NEH-guh-tiv SPAYS) The space between the parts of a drawing.

perspective (per-SPEK-tiv) A method of drawing in which near objects are shown larger than faraway objects to give an impression of depth.

pose (POHZ) The position assumed by a figure.

rigging (RIG-ing) The ropes that hold a ship's sail up.

silhouette (sih-luh-WET) A drawing that shows only a flat dark shape, like a shadow.

sketchbook (SKECH-buhk) A book in which quick drawings are made.

vanishing point (VA-nish-ing POYNT) The place in a perspective drawing where parallel lines appear to meet.

Index

A
Avery, Henry 16

B
Blackbeard 14, 15
Bonnet, Stede 16
bowsprit 22
buccaneer 20

C
charcoal 8, 10
composition 23
cross-hatching 11

F
felt-tips 9, 10
flags 16, 17, 23

H
hats 12—15, 21, 27, 30, 31

J
Jolly Roger 16, 17, 23

L
light 11, 13, 19, 21, 25, 27, 31

M
masts 22

N
negative space 17

P
paint 8, 9
paper 10
parrot 24, 25
pastel 8
pencil 8
perspective 6, 7, 22

R
Rackham, Calico Jack 17
rigging 23, 30, 31
Roberts, Bartholemew 16

S
sails 23

shade 11, 13, 19, 21, 25, 27, 29, 31
ships 12, 16, 22, 23, 26, 28, 29
shoes 15, 19, 21, 27
silhouette 10

T
Tew, Thomas 16

V
vanishing point 6, 7, 22

W
watercolor 8
weapons 14—17, 20, 21, 23, 26, 27, 30

Web Sites

Due to the changing nature of Internet links, PowerKids Press has developed an online list of Web sites related to the subject of this book. This site is updated regularly. Please use this link to access the list:

www.powerkidslinks.com/htd/pirates/